BETTER CHILDREN'S SERMONS

BOOKS BY BUCKY DANN
PUBLISHED BY THE WESTMINSTER PRESS

Better Children's Sermons:
*54 Visual Lessons, Dialogues, and
Demonstrations*

Creating Children's Sermons:
51 Visual Lessons

BETTER CHILDREN'S SERMONS

54 Visual Lessons, Dialogues, and Demonstrations

by
BUCKY DANN

THE WESTMINSTER PRESS
Philadelphia

Book Design by Alice Derr

First edition

Published by The Westminster Press®
Philadelphia, Pennsylvania

PRINTED IN THE UNITED STATES OF AMERICA
9 8 7 6 5 4 3 2 1

Library of Congress Cataloging in Publication Data

Dann, Bucky, 1951–
  Better children's sermons.

  Includes index.
  1. Children's sermons—Outlines. I. Title.
BV4315.D32 1983   252'.53   83–6851
ISBN 0–664–24481–5 (pbk.)

For Pamela
my wife and good friend

CONTENTS

INTRODUCTION   *11*

  Technique   *20*

LESSONS

INTRODUCTIONS AND SEPARATIONS

  1. Hello   *25*
  2. Going Away   *26*
  3. Farewell   *27*

PEACE

  4. Peacemakers   *28*
  5. The Peace Sign   *30*
  6. Peace in Me   *32*

LOVE OF SELF AND OTHERS

  7. I Love Me   *34*
  8. Mirror, Mirror   *36*
  9. Being Needy   *38*
  10. Good to My Body   *40*
  11. Ask for It   *42*
  12. To Hug or Not to Hug   *44*
  13. The Patience Test   *46*

THE NATURE OF GOD

14. Magnetic Love   48
15. God Loves Little People   50
16. Gift Giver   52

THE NATURE OF JESUS

17. God's Valentine   54
18. God Is Like . . .   56
19. God's Self-Portrait   58
20. God's Face   59

THE MEANING OF CHRISTMAS

21. Happy Birthday to Jesus   60
22. Baby Jesus   61

THE MEANING OF EASTER

23. The Easter Cheer   63
24. The Easter Balloon   64

RESPONSIBILITIES TO PARENTS

25. Go   66
26. Stop   68
27. Leaving Home   69

DISCIPLESHIP

28. To Tell the Truth   71
29. The Path   73
30. These Bones   75
31. Do You Trust Me?   77
32. Blindman's Buff   79

WORSHIP

33. Praise God   81
34. Sing a Song   83
35. Praying   84
36. The Treasure Chest   86
37. Kneeling Like Wise Men   88

MARRIAGE

38. The First Wedding   90
39. Promises, Promises   92

COVENANTS

40. The Handshake   94
41. God Never Forgets   96
42. The Old Deal   98
43. The New Deal   100
44. Our Father   102
45. Dead or Alive?   104
46. The Rainbow   106

BAPTISM

47. Getting Clean   107
48. Getting Watered   109
49. One of Us   111

COMMUNION

50. In Remembrance   113
51. The Greatest Gift   115
52. The Body   117
53. The Blood   119
54. Heavenly Food   121

INDEX/Scripture Passages   123

INTRODUCTION

"They wouldn't let us speak our native language or use our native names. Whenever we did, we were punished." That is how a Native American remembers his childhood experience of Christianity in a parochial school. He is now an adult who sees all of Christianity through the eyes of an angry child and whose alienation from the church is complete.

A different man tells that his son will play hymns whenever he sits down at a piano. What makes this remarkable to the father is that his son is an avowed nonbeliever and strictly a scientist. With a piano, however, the adult scientist releases his inner child and relives his childhood years in church.

Another man says his first direct encounter with God occurred during early adolescence. As a child he learned that God forgives those who ask in prayer. Suffering from guilt, he asked God to forgive him and he felt immediate, physical relief. He traces his deep spiritual interest and faith back to that first brush with God.

Each of these examples reflects, in different ways, the tremendous influence that childhood has upon a person's religious life. An adult's faith or lack of faith, and attitude toward Christ and church, are directly linked to that person's learnings and experiences as a child. Some children are blessed by finding religious meaning, a discovery that always alters their lives. Other people, like the piano player, feel drawn to a part of life they have left. They are returning from a barren space to a remembered, magical time of childhood. There are also tragedies, such as that of the Native American whose childhood experiences result in estrangement from Christianity because of the church's neglect or ineptitude. All persons, in their own way, will find themselves among these men, demonstrating the impact of childhood upon adult spirituality.

This influence exists in our religious lives because childhood is just beneath the surface of all adult behavior. Indeed, the child lives on in the adult psyche, involved in a maturing process that is far more immense and fearsome than commonly realized. The linkage may be disguised, or immediately apparent, but the childhood likes, fears, and prejudices are always very much present. Childhood establishes a program of values and habits that adults generally live without question.

Here is sufficient reason to be concerned about the Christian, spiritual input received by children, for the religious meanings and actions fixed in their childhood will commonly be maintained. Boys who attend church but whose fathers do not will usually diminish or cease their church involvement as they enter adulthood. Adults have difficulty switching from the denomination of their childhood, even when their minds tell them the difficulty is not reasonable. Many people who attended worship as children continue to attend as adults, but its deeper meaning for their lives can often be questioned and their attendance understood as the living out of childhood patterns. Along with the three men already mentioned, these are all examples of learned behavior which is universal, complex, and tremendously important.

Although these patterns can seem uncomfortably

mechanistic, they must not be ignored or resisted. They are inevitable, and are formed from whatever input a child receives. Families, churches, peer groups, and society all foster patterns of behavior and help to determine the value given to each. While children are adopting a religious pattern, they are also learning about other powers and sources of help, with corresponding models for behavior. There is intense competition.

An unfortunate result of that competition, and of the church's frequent neglect of ministries to children, is the development of Christian models that children do not highly value, as evidenced by those churches which receive many new members through a Sunday school/confirmation class system, only to see those members disappear as they reach adulthood. Many of these adults, who as children were brought into the church through this system, demonstrate a greater trust in nation, money, and other people than they do in God.

These examples illustrate that the formation of a religious pattern in childhood is not the same as a religiously significant childhood. A religiously significant childhood partly occurs when Christianity becomes a highly valued mode of behavior. Meaningful ministry helps children establish a Christian pattern that they find useful, and will utilize. That does not happen when ministries to children are disregarded, limited to Sunday school or catechism classes or done without an effective technique. An understanding of behavior patterns, and the linkage between adulthood and childhood, reveals the powerful impact this ministry will have upon individuals and the church when done well.

Ministry to children must have several components to be highly effective. Teaching by laity and clergy must focus upon a child's needs, offering help in a way that the child can comprehend. Lessons in the classroom and the sanctuary are largely wasted unless they are practical and communicate about important issues in a child's life. Children need to participate in at least part of the congregation's weekly worship. Inclusion or exclusion in worship is nothing less than inclusion or exclusion in the body of Christ, with the accompanying messages about personal importance and acceptance. That also means inclusion in Communion, the bonding ritual. Pastors need to express interest and care by spending time teaching children during worship. Children come to value this time with their pastor. Children also may be encouraged to give during worship, not just receive. Singing in choirs, ushering, and giving offerings and prayers are all practical suggestions that only depend upon a child's age or willingness. The lessons in this book are designed to assist in these ministries to children through teaching, worship, Communion, and pastoral involvement.

But a religiously significant childhood does not simply mean learning a valued behavior pattern. That becomes hollow behavior unless the roots of a deeper purpose are nourished. Children must be brought to Christ; they must be offered an opportunity to encounter God. It is this encounter which provides the purpose and power in Christianity. Without a personal experience and personal relationship with God in Christ, Christianity becomes the unthinking behavior which is the danger of our innate obedience to patterns. As Paul says, Christ gives the body a mind, Christ is its head. Without Christ, Christianity and Christians are mindless, purposeless, and empty.

Children must be brought to the presence of God through ministry. Do it carefully. The way that children are introduced to God greatly determines the God they will know. Children must be brought to God only in a manner consistent with who God is. The importance of that cannot be overemphasized.

God is in Jesus. God becomes concretely personal in Jesus, and children can understand God only in that way. Though it may seem simplistic for those who are more theologically sophisticated, let Jesus be God.

God is love. That truth cannot be taught by the use of techniques that are designed to scare children to God or that make God threatening. Evangelism and fear work against each other, because there is no fear in love. Instead, communicate the acceptance, concern, forgiveness, and gifts God has for the children. Use Jesus as a picture of that message.

With that background, teach children to trust God, to approach God, and to talk with God. Again, especially for children, this means trusting Jesus, approaching Jesus, and talking to Jesus. Do not only tell why, also show how —be practical. Help children to verbalize their fears, their guilts, and their needs to Jesus.

Give children an opportunity to do that. The turmoil in a child is as great, or greater, than in any adult. With the right preparation, children can responsibly talk to Christ in silent, personal prayer. Their prayers can be specific or open-ended, asking Christ for a certain type of help or asking Christ into their lives as a loving, constant companion and a forgiving parent. Make sure they have a clear idea of what to pray, leave them free to do it if they wish, and be assured that Christ will come.

Helping children to establish a valued pattern for behavior and to encounter Christ personally are both necessary and important. Neither one should be emphasized at the other's expense. Emphasizing models for behavior while neglecting a personal experience of God leads to hollowness. But children are also shortchanged by an overemphasis on their personal relationship with Christ, because behavior patterns are not automatically instilled or transformed by an encounter with Christ. Whatever patterns came to be valued during childhood will be the ones brought into a person's spiritual life. The patterns may then be altered, but the most spiritual and committed of Christians continue to struggle with the non-Christian behavior patterns they learned and valued as children.

One of these patterns, which becomes an obstacle in a person's emotional and spiritual life, is to think and see from a fragmented mind-set. Instead of approaching life as unified beings, people deal with life as a varied collection of distinct responses, choosing which behavior model suits the situation. The results are people with sharply divided thoughts, values, and actions within themselves. Distinctions are made between church and world, spirituality and practicality, child and adult—distinctions that develop into barriers. One segment is prevented from touching another. Contradictions are incorporated into rational behavior.

This pattern of division is as prevalent in the church as in secular society. Fragmenting practices, such as the church's separation of child and adult, unwittingly introduce these barriers into our religious lives. Sunday school is regarded as being for children, and children are made its focus. Worship is regarded as being for adults, and so it is focused on adults. Christians learn that this goes here and that goes there; child goes here and adult goes there; religion goes here and the rest of life goes over there. The separation and segregation enforced within the church are planted in Christians from the time they are small.

The fruits of this fragmentation are very important for

the church, and many of the contemporary church's deepest problems cannot be remedied until the pattern is addressed. For example, the mysterious and symbolic rituals of Baptism and Communion appeal mostly to the child. The child is the person to whom symbolism speaks. But by normally excluding the child, physically and emotionally, reserving worship and the Sacraments for the adult, most adults eventually experience these rituals as meaningless. In a larger way, that has resulted in the present-day degeneration of symbols and the symbolic.

The separating of adult and child becomes exceedingly serious if Jesus truly meant that a person must be like a child to enter the Kingdom of God. Jesus did mean it, of course, which also says that fragmentation blocks people spiritually. The adult mind has frequent difficulties with a faith that does not always appear to be rational; neither does it adequately respond to experiences of need, fear, guilt, trust, joy, and awe. While rational, adult thinking is needed to correlate information and to make decisions about accuracy by checking other learnings, it is the child who gathers and feeds the initial input. The child grounds the adult in reality; the child is the person who correctly perceives the world. Without the child, the adult is largely blind.

The dynamics within many churches results from an imbalance of adult and child. Some churches are so dominated by the rational, adult mind that little room is given to emotion, playfulness, personal expression, or the illogical. Other congregations, however, are so dominated by a childlike mind that they are characterized by confusion, erratic growth, questionable activities, and practices that are not well thought out.

Separating child and adult also helps to enforce the pattern of separating church from daily life. When children find that the pastor, worship, Communion, and other aspects of congregational life do not include them or speak to their problems, they call on other resources for help, first as children and then as adults. Christianity, a fragment, gets put in a box and stays there.

To avoid these fruits, the church must stop splitting child and adult, but must engage them with each other instead. This is begun by physically bringing adult and child together and including children in elements from which they were previously restricted. Involving children in Communion, sermons, pastoral care, and part of worship communicates that these elements are not meant for only part of a person but for all of a person and for all people. Children who are included are more likely, when they become adults, to find deeper meaning in these various aspects of worship and faith, because their inner child will be actively engaged. As well, when a sermon or part of worship is designed for children, it will appeal to the child within everyone. When adults say they enjoy the children's message, the service has begun to reach the whole person.

This may seem like a lot of meaning to hang upon some basically simple ministries, but one of the mistakes that churches make is to underestimate the importance of childhood and ministry to children. Occurrences in childhood can have an impact far out of proportion to their significance at the time. Involving children, communicating their importance, and speaking to their problems will have lifelong meaning. Since worship is the body's central celebration, it is essential that the children's involvement begin here. Since Communion is the central ritual in worship, it is necessary that children be included. Since the pastor is the church's leader, children need the pastor's attention. A children's sermon can do all of that, and do so in a way that demonstrates equality with adults.

The author of Hebrews laments that too many Christians must be bottle-fed, instead of feeding upon spiritual meat. That is less likely to happen if people are fed spiritual milk in childhood, its appropriate time in life. By providing better diets for the children, all God's people will be strengthened.

Technique

Harry Emerson Fosdick once observed that a person's mind won't absorb more than his or her seat can endure. That is a very useful axiom for anyone working with children, especially since the seats of children do not endure long sits. A child's short attention span makes it extremely important that communication be effective; there is no time to be wasted on techniques that do not work well. Children must be reached quickly, entertained, taught, and then let go.

A highly effective procedure for reaching children, discussed in *Creating Children's Sermons,* involves several strategies that are brought together into a children's lesson. Stated briefly, the technique coordinates dialogue, visualization, experiencing, and personal affection. The lessons in this book are based on these methods.

Children learn much more from what they see and experience than from what they are told. All adults can recognize their own parents in their personal behavior, displaying how effectively children learn by observation. Lessons for children, then, must provide a way for the message to be seen or visualized whenever possible. How can the lesson be physically demonstrated?

Helping children to experience the message is equally effective. Telling a child about the danger of touching a hot frying pan does not work as well as when the child is actually burned. Create a way for children to experience a lesson's main point.

Children will remember what they have experienced or seen demonstrated, so that these strategies can then be wrapped in dialogue. Ask the children questions, and allow them to ask questions. Inquire about their lives, as the lessons touch upon them, and give the children an opportunity to talk about themselves and their thoughts. The lessons are made much more personal in this way. The main points can be described in the terms and the situations they present. Even more important, a personal relationship slowly develops between the children and the leader as they grow to know one another through their dialogues. Children talk and think and know more than they are commonly given credit for; dialogue mines the real depth that children possess.

As the dialogues make the children better known, and the lessons bring leader and child together, opportunities develop for the expression of personal care, support, and acceptance. At this point, ministry has gone beyond an effort to communicate some concept and becomes a personal ministry of love and healing. Like anyone else, children need to be touched emotionally and physically, but the openness in children makes this need more apparent and makes the touch more readily received. Whenever possible, take advantage of the opportunities that the lessons will give, and touch the children with love and affirmation.

These different ingredients together comprise a highly effective technique for reaching children, which entertains and teaches on many levels. But nothing holds their attention forever, and it is important not to carry the children beyond the limits of their attention. Holding them too long in a lesson is roughly equivalent to holding a squirming child who desperately wants to escape, and is just as difficult. For most lessons, especially during worship, five to ten minutes is enough. A half hour can be managed if it is well planned. As a firm rule, however, plan not to accomplish too much.

For the same reason, there is much to commend the practice of not making young children sit through an entire worship service. Many adults think there is something beneficial about forcing a small child to endure forty or forty-five minutes of worship, not geared to children, in a state of quiet stillness that is alien to their natures. It is more likely that these children will experience worship as insufferably boring and repressive, perhaps offsetting the positive input about church which the lessons try to give.

After their segment of worship is completed, including Scripture, sermon, and song, a good alternative is to release the young children to another room for continued activities on their level. This time can include prayer, Bible stories, snacks, and fun, with adult leadership and supervision. The practice also has the added benefit of allowing parents to participate better in the service, and diminishes the stream of pilgrims to the bathroom.

This planned separation may be balanced by including children in Communion and other aspects of worship that are regarded by some traditions as reserved for adults. Beliefs and practices concerning the Sacraments of Baptism and Communion vary considerably among Christian denominations. Some advocate the baptism of adults and older children only, while other denominations baptize infants and younger children as well. Some provide the options of sprinkling, pouring, or immersion, while others allow only one of these forms. The same variety is also present in Communion; some churches serve only baptized, adult members, while the Eastern Orthodox rite allows even infants at baptism to receive the wine. Views on serving the elements to children are changing in some denominations. Included in the suggestions and lessons that follow are several relating to the Sacraments, which inevitably reflect my own Methodist background. Individuals will want to adapt these suggestions to represent their own beliefs. No one lesson, of course, can present the full significance of a Sacrament. I simply hope that each may offer an aspect of truth that can be grasped by children.

On days when the Eucharist is being celebrated, a special Communion can be shared with the children. When they are gathered in front of the sanctuary, lead them in a lesson about the Sacrament. Before pursuing the lesson, however, tell the children what is about to happen. Explain that it is a special and serious activity; they should be quieter today. I have never had a child misbehave during Communion, or treat the ceremony with disrespect. They sense that this is something special and different. Because of that, the congregation has grown comfortable with what was initially nervously tolerated.

Serving the children is easier with a common cup. The presenter is able to maintain control of the wine or juice in this way, making a spill less likely. Use a cloth to wipe the rim of the cup after each sip. Some children may be uncomfortable about drinking from the same cup as another person and refuse the wine or juice, which is totally acceptable.

Communion is also a good opportunity to bring the children to the altar. The altar is another aspect of worship frequently reserved for adults without reason. That is often unintentional, being simply because children have not been invited to kneel at the railing. The altar does not have to be used, however, and the children may be served where they are sitting.

These techniques will effectively and enjoyably involve children in the worship life of a congregation. The children will receive attention from their pastor, and will, we hope, meet Christ. As a result, it is not unusual for the children to anticipate worship; Christianity has become important for them. Those are fruits to be celebrated!

BETTER
CHILDREN'S
SERMONS

INTRODUCTIONS
AND SEPARATIONS

1. Hello

Theme: Introducing yourself to new children.

First impressions are very important. The first lesson with new children must provide an introduction and also set the tone for your future relationship. Have fun and be friendly.

Scripture: Ephesians 1:1

Device: A dialogue

Goals: To introduce yourself
To create warmth and friendliness
To establish your availability and humanity

Technique: Paul begins his letter by introducing himself. That is the purpose for this lesson. Point out to the children the connection between the Scripture and what you are doing.

Have the children guess the answers to certain questions about you. In revealing the answers, you will also give them facts about who you are. Begin with an easy one—"Am I a boy or a girl?" This provides a humorous and fun start. Have them guess your name and your age. Other questions could be about your weight, your marital status, the pets you have and their names, or the number of persons in your family. Let this be fun.

Notes: Have the children say their names to you.

2. Going Away

Theme: Preparing for a departure or separation.

Many people deal with saying good-by by not saying it. That is a great mistake, for a meaningful good-by is necessary to provide a healthy end to a relationship. People must prepare for the parting by acknowledging and accepting the coming separation. Children, like everyone else, also need preparation for the coming break.

Scripture: Ecclesiastes 3:6

Device: An apple

Goals: To prepare for a separation
To teach what separation means

Technique: Interpret for the children the meaning of the verse in Ecclesiastes. There is a time when we find each other and get together, and a time when we must lose each other and go away. Tell them that the time when you must go away is coming soon. Have the children ever had the experience of feeling sad when a person or a pet left them? You can share with them an occasion when this happened to you. Soon you will be leaving again and feeling sad again.

With the apple demonstrate the meaning of separation. Prior to the lesson, partially cut the apple in half so that you can separate the halves easily. Pull the apple apart, describing that there are times when people must pull apart and go away from each other. They may never get together again, but they can always remember each other.

3. Farewell

Theme: Saying good-by to children you have known.

Saying good-by is difficult. Words do not always communicate what you want to say, because it is impossible to summarize all that has happened in a relationship. Nonverbal gestures can often say more, and be more satisfying.

Scripture: 2 Corinthians 13:11

Device: Gestures

Goals: To say a meaningful good-by
To communicate caring

Technique: This lesson is designed to say good-by without using words. Three different gestures, done in a series, will communicate your love for the children, encouragement to stay close to God, and your feelings of pain at leaving. The last gesture is taken from the movie *E.T.* The creature in the movie, unable to speak English, says good-by with a touching expression of love and sadness.

After reading the Scripture, signal the children to be quiet by touching your finger to your lips. Point to yourself, rub your heart, and point to each of them. Point to the sky, to the Bible, to the children, and then hug the Bible. Touch your finger to your heart, to your lips, and hold your fingertip out to them, quietly saying, "Ouch." Close by shaking each child's hand and saying good-by.

Notes: If you know sign language, you could substitute that for these gestures.

PEACE

4. Peacemakers

Theme: Jesus tells us not to kill our enemies.

How to respond to an enemy is a surprisingly personal issue, because it touches upon some of our most basic fears. But the teachings of Jesus are clear and straightforward. Love of our enemies is called for, and peacemakers are exalted. It is important that children hear this message in a world where war is falsely justified, love is twisted to mean violence, and murder is tragically common. Nonviolence is not the message of some fuzzy idealists; it is the message of God's Word in the New Testament.

Scripture: Matthew 5:44

Device: A toy gun

Goals: To teach God's opposition to violence
To teach the danger of weapons
To plant seeds for future fruit

Technique: As the children what an enemy is. How do enemies act? Do they have any enemies? This may be a time when the children share some bad experiences they have had. Do they feel angry toward their enemies? Let the children know that you can identify with their anger.

Sometimes adults get so angry with their enemies that they kill them. Hold up the toy gun. Have the children heard about anyone being killed with a gun? Every year many people kill others with guns. Guns kill many people in wars.

Would Jesus think it is good or bad to kill an enemy with a gun? After they have given their answers, reread the Scripture passage. Is killing an enemy a way of loving that enemy? Instead of killing our enemies, Jesus tells us to pray and ask God to help our enemies stop doing bad things. Jesus tells us to put away our guns.

We may feel angry, but we must never kill an enemy. That's what Jesus says in the Bible. Rather than kill, Jesus wants us to talk to God about our enemies, and help our enemies to stop being bad.

5. The Peace Sign

Theme: Jesus wants us to be peacemakers.

Worldwide peace will not occur magically. It must begin in little ways, in our daily relationships, which are far too often controlled by hostility. The peacemakers whom Jesus blesses are not necessarily diplomats and rulers on the world stage, but are those who work to make peace in their own small space.

Scripture: Matthew 5:9

Device: The American Indian sign of peace

Goals: To teach the importance of peace
To give a simple way of making peace

Technique: A well-known symbol of peace is the American Indian whose open hand is held up to the world. The open, uplifted hand contains no aggression and holds no weapons. It is the opposite of the clenched fist, which symbolizes hostility and hatred. Use these two opposite symbols to demonstrate the nature of peace to the children, and to give them a means of practicing peace.

Show the children the sign of peace, asking them if they know what it is. If they don't know, explain what the uplifted hand means and some of its background. It's a sign of peace. Then show them a fist. Ask if that is a sign of peace or of fighting. Emphasize the difference between the two ways of holding the hand.

Remind the children of the Beatitude. Whom does Jesus bless, the fighter or the peacemaker? How would Jesus want us to hold our hands? Show the children the two ways and let them decide. Affirm their correct choice and let them practice the sign. Before you stop the lesson, have them hold up their open hands and tell each other "Peace." That is what Jesus wants.

Notes: You could ask the children to let this sign, accompanied by saying "Peace," be how you greet each other.

6. Peace in Me

Theme: Peace begins inside us.

Peace is an extremely difficult achievement. It demands the hardest aspects of love, as Paul describes love in 1 Corinthians: patience, not seeking our own, not remembering wrongs, bearing all things. We should not expect peace to occur easily or quickly in ourselves, let alone in the world. Instead, we should work upon being peaceful in ourselves by loving ourselves.

Scripture: John 14:27

Device: A meditation

Goals: To teach the importance of inner peace
To teach a means of finding inner peace
To provide positive reinforcement for the children

Technique: Begin by talking to the children about anger. Have they ever seen an angry person? What do angry people do? Explain to the children that sometimes people can get angry with themselves as well as with other people. We can call ourselves names. We can think we're dumb or ugly or weak. We wish we could do some things better. Jesus says we can be happy and peaceful, but to do that we must stop being angry with ourselves.

Tell the children you will show them something to do, when they become angry, that will help them be more peaceful and happier. Instruct the children in the following short meditation. Have them take two deep breaths, then tell them to sit quietly and listen to the sounds around them. After a few moments, say the following sentence, "God made me; I am good," and have the children repeat it out loud twice. Then have the children shut their eyes and say it to themselves.

Explain that they can do this whenever they're feeling angry with themselves or with someone else. It is a way of making peace inside us.

Notes: Do not go through this process too quickly; allow adequate time for the children to adjust and adopt each of the three segments. However, pay attention to the children and move along when it seems appropriate, not dwelling too long on any particular part. Otherwise, you will encourage giggling and other disruptive actions.

LOVE OF SELF AND OTHERS

7. I Love Me

Theme: We are to love ourselves.

Funny as it seems, loving ourselves is very difficult. The difficulty stems from a tragic conclusion, made during childhood, enforced by traditional theology, that something is wrong with ourselves. We decide we are not worth loving. But Jesus and Paul teach differently. Loving ourselves is acceptable and necessary. We are free to develop this ability.

Scripture: Galatians 5:14

Device: The use of imitation

Goals: To give permission to love self
To teach some ways to love self
To experience self-love

Technique: State that both Jesus and Paul say we are to love others and that we are also to love ourselves. How can we love ourselves? Do they have any ideas?

Ask the children how people can show love to each other. List their answers: give gifts, hug, kiss, etc. Use the list to inform the children that they may also do these things for themselves. It is O.K. to give yourself a gift. It is O.K. to give yourself a compliment.

Have the children ever kissed themselves? Show them how, kissing yourself up and down your arm. Tell them to do it too, and let it be fun. Have they ever hugged themselves? Wrap your arms around yourself and give yourself a big hug. Have the children do this also. Conclude by reminding the children that Jesus teaches us to love ourselves. Anytime we wish, we can give ourselves a hug.

Notes: Over a year after I had used this message my daughter was giving herself hugs one morning at breakfast. I'd forgotten about the lesson, but she hadn't. Don't underestimate a lesson's importance or a child's ability to remember

8. Mirror, Mirror

Theme: We are to love ourselves, as well as others.

In the two great commandments affirmed by Jesus we are told to love God, our neighbors, and ourselves. Christianity has commonly neglected love of self, emphasizing love for God and other people instead. That is a harmful prejudice which needs to be corrected. Love of self is a great need, and our ability to follow much of what Jesus teaches will depend upon our ability to love ourselves.

Scripture: Matthew 22:37–39

Device: A mirror

Goals: To teach the acceptability of self-love
To encourage the children to love themselves
To equate the importance of love for neighbors with the importance of love for self

Technique: Ask the children what important word is repeated several times in the Scripture passage. Have them listen for the word as you read the verses again. What three people does Jesus tell us to love? We are to love God, our neighbors, and ourselves.

Have the children name some persons whom they love. Why do they love these persons? After discussing these loves, hold a mirror before the face of a child and ask the child if he or she loves that person in the mirror. Show the mirror to every child, asking each the same question. Don't be surprised if many of the children say no. As you go around, distribute compliments and support. Now is a good opportunity to express love and lift up egos. Explain to the children that Jesus says we can love that person in the mirror. Jesus wants you to love you. The next time the children look in the mirror they are to like that wonderful person they see.

Notes: It is amazing how early children learn not to love themselves, or that it is wrong to do so.

9. Being Needy

Theme: We each have needs.

Being human means having needs. When our needs are not met, we suffer or die; when our needs are fulfilled, we live and grow and find happiness. Before we can begin to meet our needs, however, we must first recognize that we have them.

Scripture: Psalm 109:22

Device: A plant that needs to be potted; a pot; soil; water

Goals: To teach what personal needs are
To teach that people have needs
To teach the importance of meeting needs

Technique: The plant, in this lesson, will serve as a picture of what needs are and why we must meet them. The plant will be like a person.

Personal needs are an abstract concept. Children may not know what is meant until you demonstrate with the plant. Ask the children what a need is. Do they have any? Don't be surprised if they do not know what you mean. Show them the plant out of the soil with bare roots. Does the plant need anything? This type of need the children can visualize and understand.

What does the plant need? The children probably will know that it needs soil and water. As they specify each need, supply it for the plant. What would happen to the plant if it wasn't potted in soil and watered? What would happen to the plant if these needs were not met? It would die, of course. After you have potted the plant, ask the children if the plant needs anything else. Don't be surprised if they say that the plant needs love. Affirm that the plant does need love, and stroke one of the leaves.

Draw the parallel between the plant and the children. They have needs, just as the plant does. What might their needs be? This time they will have ideas. They need food. They need water. Do they need love too? Point out to the children that if they do not get food or water or love, they will be unhappy or die, just as the plant would. We all have needs. As the Bible says, we are needy people.

Notes: There is evidence that plants do respond to personal attention and loving care through words and touching.

10. Good to My Body

Theme: We are to take care of our bodies.

One aspect of love is to care for people's needs. That is also true about loving ourselves. We are to care for ourselves. Self-abuse is evidence that self-love is lacking. This is especially apparent with our bodies. In love, we will care for our bodies and keep them healthy. They are an important and wonderful part of us. Without love, we allow our bodies and ourselves to deteriorate.

Scripture: 1 Corinthians 3:16–17

Device: An empty beer bottle; a pack of cigarettes; a toothbrush; a milk carton

Goals: To teach how to love ourselves
To teach ways we abuse ourselves
To support abstinence from personal abuse

Technique: Explain to the children part of what Paul means in this Scripture passage. We are to take care of our bodies and keep them healthy, because they are special. What are some good things we can do for our bodies? What are some bad things we may do to our bodies? What happens when we are bad to our bodies? We often become sick. When we go out in the cold without a coat and then become sick, it is our own fault. When we sit in the sun too long and get burned, it is our own fault. We weren't being good to our bodies.

Tell the children you have some examples of good and bad things. Have the children identify the various objects and whether they are good or bad for our bodies. With the children's help, explain what is good or bad about each object.

God wants us to love ourselves and be good to our bodies. Hold up the good objects and affirm that God wants us to use these things. God does not want us to do things that are bad for our bodies or that make us sick. Hold up the bad objects and affirm that God does not want us to use these.

Notes: Vary the objects according to what is appropriate in your community.

Point out the label on the pack of cigarettes which announces how harmful they are.

The children may talk about their parents' habits during the dialogue.

11. Ask for It

Theme: Ask for what you want.

This very simple technique for satisfying our needs and desires is not easy to do. We are inhibited about asking for things or making requests of people. Jesus had no such difficulty. He frequently asked people for what he wanted and teaches us to do the same. Asking is the most straightforward way of doing business and prevents manipulation.

Scripture: Matthew 7:7

Device: A piece of bubble gum for each child

Goals: To teach a technique for meeting our needs
To support those who already ask for things
To have fun

Technique: Make some requests of the children after they have gathered together. Start with silly requests so that the children pay attention to what you are doing, instead of focusing upon what you are asking for. Ask different children if they will give their shirt, or shoe, or sock, or pants to you. Do this in a fun way so that the children know you are kidding. After the children are paying attention, ask them what you are doing. Pick up on the word "ask." Explain that you are asking for things.

Read the Scripture to the children. What does Jesus tell us to do? He tells us to ask for what we want. What are some things the children ask for? Do they ask their parents or their friends for anything? Jesus says it is good to ask. Asking is a good way to get what we want.

Though we may not always get it, asking is always a good idea.

Show the bubble gum to the children. How many of them like bubble gum? What would Jesus say is a good thing to do if you want some gum? The answer should be obvious. We need to ask. Their requests will naturally follow. Hand out gum to the children as they ask for it. Repeat the message: Jesus tells us to ask for what we want.

Notes: Be sure you have enough gum for all the children. Give gum last to those who do not ask, repeating the message for them.

Emphasize that the pieces of gum are to be taken home unopened and unused.

12. To Hug or Not to Hug

Theme: Sometimes love means letting go.

Hugs are a common way of showing love and affection. But love can also mean the opposite, knowing when to let go and not hold someone. Unless this is recognized, an expression of care can become a tool for imprisoning or using a person. Part of love's meaning is letting go.

Scripture: Ecclesiastes 3:5

Device: A child from your group

Goals: To teach part of love's meaning
To support the children's desires not to be held sometimes
To help experience love as letting go

Technique: If you hold a child long enough, he or she will begin to squirm and make very clear the desire to be released. This is a metaphor for situations all human beings find themselves in at times, and can be used to demonstrate the lesson's point.

Ask if the children understand the meaning of the word "embrace." Talk about embraces as hugs. Who gives them hugs? Can they demonstrate? A hug is a sign of love. But love also means not hugging sometimes. That's what was read in the Scripture: a time for hugging and a time for not hugging. Have they ever wanted not to be held or hugged? When?

Choose an active child to demonstrate your meaning. Give the child a hug and then say you are not going to let go. Even if the child wants to get away, you're going to hold on. This will probably be enough to start the child struggling to escape. If not, challenge the child to escape. Hold on, don't let go. As you hold on, explain to the children that sometimes love means not hugging. If someone wants to get away, the loving thing to do is to let that person go and not hang on. Let the child run free.

Notes: The children will know what you are talking about, though they may not express themselves greatly. This is a problem they commonly experience.

13. The Patience Test

Theme: Patience is waiting for what we want.

Paul says that love is patient. This means enduring and waiting for what we want, though we may feel frustrated, silly, or hurt in the process. That is part of love. Patience allows time for love to work. Love cannot be hurried and so gives space to others.

Scripture: 1 Corinthians 13:4

Device: Pieces of bubble gum; a chair

Goals: To teach the meaning of patience
　　　　 To reward patience

Technique: Along with a verbal definition of patience, children need a physical example. This will be supplied by a child being tested for patience.

Ask what child would like to win a piece of bubble gum. Explain that the child must first pass a patience test to get the gum. From the volunteers, pick a child for the patience test. The child must sit in a chair, with the eyes covered, until you say to stop. The gum is the prize if the child does that without peeking. Place the volunteer in the chair, telling the other boys and girls to make sure the child doesn't peek, then proceed with the lesson.

Involve the remaining children by asking what the word "patience" means. Don't be surprised if the children understand the term well. What are some of the times they lose their patience? Christmas is a good example of a time when children lose patience; they want to open their packages. During the discussion, check the child in the chair. Has the child peeked? Point out to the children that the child's patience is being tested.

Have all the children who have brothers or sisters raise their hands. Are those children always able to maintain their patience with their brother or sister? What happens when they lose their patience? The children may talk about having a toy taken from them and the ensuing fight. In that situation, what would be the patient thing to do? Paul says that love is patient. Love will wait for the toy to be given back.

Turn to the child in the chair. Are the eyes still covered? Has the child been patient? Ask the rest of the children; let them answer. Award the gum, commending the child's patience. State clearly that God rewards people who are patient.

Notes: If the child becomes impatient and peeks, ask the other children whether that is patience or impatience. After their answer, choose another child or give the same one another chance.

If you have enough gum, you can try the test on all the children at once. This would change the lesson's dialogue, but could have some interesting results.

You may want to have enough gum for all the children anyway, so that no one is left out on the goodies. Stress that the pieces of gum are to be taken home unopened and unused.

THE NATURE OF GOD

14. Magnetic Love

Theme: God searches and finds those who are lost.

Being lost is a universal human experience, and all people know its attending feelings of fear and sadness. Much of this parable's impact is drawn from these feelings and experiences. God searches for those who have strayed from him and find themselves lost in life. Nothing holds God back from his search, until he is able to rejoice at having found his precious creature.

Scripture: Matthew 18:12–14

Device: A magnet; one small magnetic object; many small nonmagnetic objects; a dish

Goals: To demonstrate God's love
To communicate the security found in God

Technique: A magnet is a very mysterious tool. It uses an invisible power to accomplish some remarkable results. As such, a magnet becomes a fine symbol of God and can be used to re-create this parable for the children.

Begin by putting the children in touch with the meaning of being lost. Have any of them ever been lost? Let them describe some of the times; you may also share with them a time when you were lost. How did it feel to be lost? Discuss the parable with them. What had happened to this sheep? What was the shepherd doing? Did he find his sheep? That story shows us what God is like. God is like the shepherd and we are like the sheep. Sometimes we wander away from God. We stop coming to church, we stop reading the Bible, we stop praying. Whenever we wander away from God, and become lost, God will search for us until he finds us.

Show the children the small magnetic object, then mix it in the dish with the nonmagnetic objects. Each one of us is like that small object, because we easily become lost in everything that's all around us. Let the children look in the dish. Can they find the lost "person"? Holding up the magnet, explain that God will come searching for us. Move the magnet over the small objects in the dish. Only the small magnetic object will be picked up by the magnet. Hold the magnet up with the object stuck to it. Just like this magnet, God searches for us until he finds us. Demonstrate with the magnet again.

Notes: The best small objects to use are ones that look alike, although they differ in their ability to be magnetic. Screws, for example, can look just alike but be made from different metals. This way the children will not be able to tell which object you placed in the bowl, making for a greater simulation of that object being lost.

A large magnet makes a better symbol of God than a small one.

15. God Loves Little People

Theme: God loves children.

Our churches frequently treat children as if they are less important in the eyes of God. They cannot do what adults can to build up the church or sustain it. But God is clear about his concern and affection for them. Several times we are told not to discount children and to treat them with importance. God loves them.

Scripture: Matthew 18:10

Device: Some adult clothes, such as shoes, coat, pants, and hat

Goals: To communicate God's love for children
To confirm them in this love
To communicate their importance

Technique: This lesson endeavors to affirm the smallness of children by making it a quality God loves. That not only teaches about God's love but also makes children important.

After reading the Scripture, ask the children how big God is. Affirm their attempts to answer, and tell them that God is even bigger. Yet it says in this verse that God loves little people, even though God is so big. That's wonderful. But if God is going to love little people, then we have to find some little people for God to love. What is a little person? Do the children know any? Let them think of themselves. If God loves little people, and they're little, then God must love them. That makes them very special.

Tell the children that you have a test that will determine who is a little person. You have some clothes of big people which won't fit little people. That's how we can tell who is a real little person whom God loves. Have the children try on different clothes. When the clothes are too big, it means they have passed the test. They are real little people. God loves them. They are very special.

Notes: Find some large clothes.

16. Gift Giver

Theme: God gives gifts to each of us.

Paul thanks God for his unspeakable gift. Scripture tells of many such gifts from God, who gives to us freely and generously. The love of God can be seen in these gifts, gifts that are beyond comprehension.

Scripture: 2 Corinthians 9:15

Device: A box wrapped with gift wrap; items of your choosing to signify the enclosed gift

Goals: To teach that God gives gifts
To make those gifts tangible
To help the children feel expectant about their gifts

Technique: This lesson can be part of a series about God's gifts to us, each lesson focusing upon a different gift. Each time use the gift-wrapped package with a different item inside to symbolize that week's particular gift. Some suggestions for various divine gifts are: Jesus, world, themselves, parents, animals, Bible.

Hold up the gift-wrapped box and ask the children what you have in your hands. In the Scripture verse, who did it say gives gifts to us? Whom do they think this gift is from? Have a note on the box which reads, "To you, from God." Pass the box around and let the children read the note. Can they guess what is in the box? Let them hold it, shake it, and wonder what is inside.

Discuss with the children times when they give and receive gifts. Why do they give gifts? Did they know that God gives gifts for the same reasons? What could

God possibly give to them? Let them open the box.

When they have opened the box and found what is inside, let them identify the gift. Discuss the gift with the children and why that gift is important. Why did God give us that? God also gives us many other gifts, and next week you'll talk about another.

Notes: If you are in a situation where you know what to expect, you could take the time to wrap a small box for each child with the child's name on the tag. This would make the message even more personalized.

THE NATURE OF JESUS

17. God's Valentine

Theme: God sent Jesus to tell us that he loves us.

It is so important for people to realize that God loves them. The message can never be repeated too many times. Continually our minds envision a divine love that is conditional or filled with harshness. Jesus, however, reveals that God's love is unconditional and without limits. Jesus brings us that message from God.

Scripture: John 3:16

Device: A valentine

Goals: To teach that Jesus is a gift of love
To teach that God loves us
To teach that God sent Jesus

Technique: This lesson is very simple. A child's experience of Valentine's Day is used to show the purpose and nature of Jesus.

Hold up a valentine, letting the children identify what you have. Ask what valentines are used for. Do they send valentines? Do they receive valentines? Why? Discuss valentines and their purpose. When the purpose is clear, explain that Jesus is a valentine. Who might have sent this valentine? When the children have answered, repeat the message. Jesus is a valentine, a love note, sent to us from God. God sent Jesus to tell us that he loves us. Read the

Scripture and repeat those important words: "God so loved the world that he sent his only Son."

Notes: This lesson will work best around Valentine's Day. You can hand out valentines from God to the children.

18. God Is Like . . .

Theme: Jesus helps us to see God.

In ancient times people worshiped many objects as images of God, but these lifeless representations were misleading. They did not contain any real power, they could not demonstrate God's love, and they were not accurate pictures of what God is truly like. Jesus came to correct this. He contained power, demonstrated God's love, and gave us the correct image of the invisible God.

Scripture: Colossians 1:15

Device: A rock; a stick; a plunger; a can of insect spray; any other object you choose

Goals: To communicate one of the purposes for Christ's life

To demonstrate the necessity of the purpose

To express affection

Technique: Ask the children what special person God sent to our world a long time ago. God sent Jesus. Do they know why God sent Jesus? Listen to their answers and then tell them you're going to show them another reason. God sent Jesus to make himself visible. The only way we can see God is to look at Jesus.

Tell the children you are going to show them various objects. You want them to tell you if the objects remind them of God. Begin with the plunger. Is that like God? They'll answer no. Follow with the other objects: rock, insect spray, stick, or anything else that looks like fun. Finally, pick up one of the small children in your arms and kiss the child on the cheek. Does that seem more like

God? This is one reason why God sent Jesus to us. Jesus can show us what God is like, and nothing else can. In Jesus we can see God.

Notes: This can be a fun lesson, so leave time for laughs.

G.U.M
2/18/90

19. God's Self-Portrait

Theme: Jesus is the picture God made of himself.

God's invisible nature is one of the reasons that Jesus Christ is so important. As the author of John affirms, no one has ever seen God. Jesus came to make God known. The invisible God is made visible in Jesus, the exact representation of God's nature. Since God created Jesus, Jesus is God's intentional self-portrait.

Scripture: John 14:9

Device: An easel with newsprint and marking pens; or a chalkboard and chalk

Goals: To teach a purpose for Jesus
To teach what God is like
To experience what God did in Jesus

Technique: Focus the attention of the children upon the words of Jesus, "Whoever has seen me has seen the Father." What does Jesus mean? Whom do we see in Jesus? When we look at Jesus we see God. Jesus is a picture of God that God made for us.

Ask the children if they would like to draw pictures of themselves on the newsprint or the chalkboard. Let as many children do this as you have space and time. After they have finished, explain that they have drawn a picture of themselves which all of us can see. That is what God did in Jesus. Jesus is the picture God drew of himself, just as they drew themselves on the paper. We can look on the paper and see the child; we can look at Jesus and see God.

20. God's Face

Theme: Jesus is God's face.

Jesus is the visible image of the invisible God, the exact likeness of God's nature. In Jesus we can observe God in the form of a human being. This basic Christian doctrine says that one of the primary purposes for Jesus is to give God a face.

Scripture: Hebrews 1:3

Device: A mask

Goals: To teach who Jesus is
To teach how we can see God

Technique: Masks are a favorite toy for children, and they know how a mask can change the appearance of the person who wears it. Jesus is a mask for God, giving a faceless God a face.

Put on the mask after reading the Scripture. The mask should be a friendly one, not one of a monster. The mask is representing Christ. The children will respond playfully to your wearing a mask; let them enjoy the unusual situation. Ask if they know who is wearing the mask. Of course they do. Ask if masks can ever get up and walk around by themselves. Of course not, masks must always be worn by somebody. Tell the children that Jesus was a mask for someone. Somebody was behind Jesus, just as you are behind that mask. Do they know who? The answer is God. Jesus is God's face.

Notes: This is a good lesson to use around Halloween.

THE MEANING OF CHRISTMAS

21. Happy Birthday to Jesus

Theme: Christmas celebrates the day that Jesus was born.

The meaning of Christmas does not need to be repeated as much as our celebrations need to be centered around that meaning. As we enjoy the season we must also remember its origin.

Scripture: Matthew 2:1

Device: A birthday cake with candles

Goals: To celebrate Christ's birth
To keep the meaning of Christmas in its celebration
To have fun

Technique: Since Christmas is the traditional birth date for Jesus, the meaning and celebration of Christmas can easily be combined with a birthday party. Have a small party for Jesus, singing "Happy Birthday" to Jesus and sharing cake. The children can blow out the candles for Jesus. Close with a joyous Christmas hymn.

Notes: This lesson works well during worship when the entire congregation can sing "Happy Birthday" to Jesus.

22. Baby Jesus

Theme: Jesus came into our world as a baby.

One of the most mind-boggling aspects of the Christian message is that God entered our world as a helpless, small, dependent infant. There is a an awesome humility in the God revealed in Christ. As well, knowing that Jesus was a real baby does much to humanize him. Although he was the incarnation of God, he was also very much like us. Too easily we can create a false separation between Jesus and the rest of humanity.

Scripture: Luke 2:6–7

Device: A baby doll or a real infant

Goals: To make the baby Jesus more real
To humanize Jesus

Technique: Even small children know about babies and are entranced with them. This will enable the children to gain an understanding of Jesus as a baby.

Cradle the infant or doll in your arms and talk to the children about babies. How many of them were babies once? How many have babies in their families? What are some of the things we need to do for babies? Can babies take care of themselves? Aim to clarify, for the children, the true situation and limitations for babies.

Turn the lesson to Jesus. How did Jesus come into the world? Was Jesus able to take care of himself when he was a baby? Do you think he cried? Did his mother change h's diapers? At Christmas we celebrate the day Jesus was born into our world as a baby.

Notes: A real infant is much more effective, of course, but if one is not available, a baby doll will suffice.

Follow this lesson with a hymn that emphasizes the baby Jesus, such as "Away in a manger."

THE MEANING OF EASTER

23. The Easter Cheer

Theme: Easter celebrates the day Jesus Christ rose from the dead.

Jesus was killed by crucifixion, but three days later he was miraculously made alive once more. In this event is found our own hope for freedom from death, with all that means. That is why Easter is a joyful celebration.

Scripture: Matthew 28:5–6

Goals: To instill the basic Easter message
To teach that Easter is a celebration
To help the children celebrate

Technique: The message and the celebration of Easter will be combined by leading the children in an Easter cheer. Discuss the events of Easter, making sure they have a basic understanding. Tell them that we celebrate Easter because it is such a wonderful thing that Jesus came alive again. Ask them to repeat the Easter words after you: "Christ is risen!" Have them say these same words. Give them permission to shout the words; this gives the message a greater feeling of jubilation and fun. Repeat "Christ is risen" three times, ending with a loud hurray. After they have done this twice, have them stand up and lead the congregation in the Easter cheer.

Notes: When the children say hurray, you can have them wave their hands in the air.

24. The Easter Balloon

Theme: Easter promises that all people will come back to life.

Easter celebrates the day when Jesus overcame death and was returned to life. According to Paul, this event was a demonstration of what will happen for all people. All will be raised to life, just as all will die.

Scripture: 1 Corinthians 15:22

Device: A balloon; a marking pen

Goals: To communicate the meaning of Easter
To affirm that all people will die
To affirm that all people will come back to life

Technique: The balloon will be used to symbolize people. This is best done by choosing one child to identify with the balloon.

Ask the children, "Who makes us alive?" They will know that God does this. Affirming their answer, ask the children to pretend the balloon is a person. Suggest that they name the balloon after a particular child, choosing one from volunteers. Blow up the balloon and make the child alive. After the balloon is inflated, draw a face on it, letting the children tell you what to draw. Shall you draw eyes? Shall you draw a nose? A big one? Do anything that makes the balloon more like a person. If you've named the balloon after a girl, for example, take someone's Easter hat and place it on the balloon.

After the balloon has been transformed, ask the children what happens to all people who have been made alive by God. They all die. All of us here will die. Let out the air and show them the deflated, wrinkled balloon. The face on the balloon will look deathly. But what happened to Jesus after he died? The children will, we hope, know this. Do they think they will come back to life too? God made Jesus alive again, and that is also what God will do to all of us. After we die, God will make each one of us alive, just like Jesus. Blow up the balloon again. This time, tie a knot at the end of the balloon. Easter promises us that we all will come back to life after we die, and never die again.

Notes: You can tie this lesson to the description of God breathing life into a human being in Genesis 2:7.

After this lesson, all the children wanted balloons. If you want to go to the expense, you may give each child a balloon.

If you have time, each child may draw his or her face on a balloon and go through the lesson together.

RESPONSIBILITIES TO PARENTS

25. Go

Theme: Children are to obey their parents.

The relationship between parent and child can often seem to be a struggle of will. Both parent and child fight each other, instead of cooperating, and both lose. Paul's teachings were designed to make the parent-child relationship one of love and mutual respect. Parents are given authority to protect and nurture children; they are not to discourage or neglect them. As a result, children are told to obey their parents.

Scripture: Ephesians 6:1

Device: A green "go" sign

Goals: To teach children obedience to their parents
To experience obedience

Technique: Make a sign with the word "go" written on it, and color the sign green. Green, of course, is a universal color for the word "go." The sign must be large enough to be easily read, but small enough to be held in your hand.

The lesson is simple, and similar to the children's game called Mother, May I. After the Scripture-reading, discuss the meaning and difficulties of obeying parents. What do the children's parents tell them to do? Do the children always obey? What happens when they don't obey? Bring the Bible passage into the discussion. What does the Bible tell us to do? We are to do what our parents say: we are to obey.

After you have talked about obedience, let the children practice it. Explain that you will tell them something to do, but they can do it only if you hold up the go sign. They must stop when you take away the sign. Lead them in some simple exercises: standing up, jumping up and down, yelling "amen," waving their hands. After a command, wait a moment before holding up the sign. Make them think before they obey. When you finish, show the children how they have acted obediently. That is what we are to do for our parents.

Notes: This lesson can also be focused upon obedience to God. A possible Scripture for that would be Jonah 3:1–2.

26. Stop

Theme: Children are to obey their parents.

Obedience of children to parents has two sides: doing what they are bidden and not doing what they are forbidden. My own childhood memories lead me to believe that the latter is more difficult.

As parents, we should also be aware of the tremendous responsibility that our authority entails. If someone is told to obey us, then we must be sure that our teachings and commands are worth being obeyed, and we must not exploit our position. That is why Paul follows his teachings about a child's duty with instructions about a parent's responsibilities.

Scripture: Colossians 3:20

Device: A red "stop" sign

Goals: To teach children obedience to their parents
To experience obedience

Technique: As in the previous lesson, make a sign, but with the word "stop" written upon it and color the sign red. The format is the same, only focus upon what the children's parents tell them not to do. Let the children practice not doing things. Instruct the children that you will tell them to do something, but they must stop when you hold up the sign. Again, make them think before they obey and then affirm their obedience.

Notes: This lesson can be done using both signs, "go" and "stop."

27. Leaving Home

Theme: God wants us to leave home someday.

Much of the tension between parent and child centers around the child's drive to be independent. The anger of early childhood and adolescence provides needed energy for the breaking-away process. This independence needs to be gradually given with wisdom, and children need affirmation about the goodness of their overall desire.

Scripture: Genesis 2:24

Device: An apple; a knife

Goals: To support children in their desire for independence

To teach that independence will happen in the future

Technique: Talk to the children about their families. How many brothers and sisters do they have? Have any brothers and sisters left home? Where did they go? For what reasons? Someday the children will leave home too. The Scripture verse says that God wants us to leave our father and mother and have our own families someday.

Show the children an apple and tell them that their families are like that apple. Cut the apple open and show them the seeds. The children are like the seeds. They live and grow up inside the apple, where it is safe and warm. But someday they will leave and go outside. What happens when these seeds leave and fall into the ground?

They make new families of apples. Those children are the same. Someday they will leave the warmth and protection of their families and have a home, family, and children of their own. That is the way God wants it.

DISCIPLESHIP

28. To Tell the Truth

Theme: We are to tell the truth.

This command from God in Zechariah is repeated by Paul in Ephesians 4:15,25. There are few commands that are more difficult. Just as with Christ's teachings that we are to love, we continually find depths of truth that go beyond what we had previously known. In the more personal sense, we continually find ways in which we have not told the truth about ourselves or the world. God's command that the truth must be told not only exalts the truth but leads us into the invaluable examination of ourselves and reality.

Scripture: Zechariah 8:16

Device: Playacting

Goals: To teach the meaning of truth
To demonstrate the meaning of lies
To encourage truth-telling

Technique: Some values, such as beauty, are best understood when their opposite is observed. That is true for truth-telling. The meaning of telling the truth is set into high relief by our observing the telling of lies.

Begin by playacting a person who lies. Don't tell the children what you are doing, but make the lies obvious ones. Let the acting be playful. Tell them your name, using a ridiculous one, and tell them you just turned five years old last week. You might tell them about your pet aardvark or about the day you caught a whale in the local pond. Use your imagination. The children, of course, will not believe you. Ask them what you are doing.

Read the Scripture and start the children thinking about God's command that we must tell the truth to each other. Ask them if you were obeying or disobeying God's command just now. Children have many struggles with this. There are many opportunities when it seems more convenient to lie. Have them discuss times they have lied, or told less than the truth. Share a moment of your own when you also lied. School test marks or broken objects are common examples. Close with a reminder of God's command. In all the examples that were just discussed, what would God have us do? God wants us to tell the truth to each other.

Notes: Sharing a time when you did not tell the truth creates a good opportunity for you to humanize yourself to the children.

Even though the playacting may be playful, become serious when discussing actual times the children have lied.

29. The Path

Theme: Jesus gives us a narrow path to follow.

Jesus says that the way to life is hard and the gate that opens to this way is narrow. The image of a path is being used. If we wish to find the life of peace, freedom, abundance, and joy, we must follow the path of Jesus. He gives us the path markers; we must follow.

Scripture: Matthew 7:14

Device: Ten or fifteen arrows or markers made of paper or cardboard

Goals: To teach what a path is
To teach what it means to follow a path
To teach that Christ gives us a path to follow

Technique: Before the service begins, use the arrows to lay out a path in the sanctuary. These arrows are easily cut out of paper. Make them large enough to be clearly seen. Place them on the floor or tape them to the walls, thus marking a path which the children can follow. Let the path begin from where you meet together and also return to that place.

Talk to the children about paths. What are paths? Have they ever followed a path? Where do they go? Tell the children that Jesus gives us a path that will lead us into a happy life, but we must first learn how to be good path followers.

Which children have followed paths before? Pick someone to lead the rest on the path you have made. This is a good chance to pick a boy or someone who normally doesn't participate. Have the children follow their leader along the path.

When they have returned, congratulate them for being good path followers. This is what we must do as Christians. Jesus teaches us how to live and what to do; we must follow him just as we followed the path this morning.

Notes: Make the path fun, but not too complicated.

30. These Bones

Theme: Children are important and belong in the church.

The New Testament consistently describes a group of believers with analogies to the human body. Although there are many parts with different functions, they are all members of the same body and work together for a larger purpose. They belong to each other and need each other. This is also true for Christians. No matter what we do for the church, each of us is important and we all belong together.

Scripture: Romans 12:4–5

Device: A cardboard skeleton

Goals: To demonstrate the nature of the church
To teach the importance of working together
To teach children they are important and belong in the church

Technique: A skeleton can depict how bodies work. It shows that bodies are made up of different parts with different functions. Children can clearly see the different bones. Begin by talking about bones. Let the children point to one of their bones. Explain that we all have bones and that there are many different kinds of bones in us: hand bones, foot bones, head bones. Do these bones all do the same things? How many of us walk on our heads or hold glasses with our feet? Our bones help us to do different things, and each bone is important. Demonstrate with the cardboard skeleton by folding the feet up or folding the head down. We can't do without any of the bones.

Draw the analogy to the church. The church is made up of many different persons and jobs. Name a few of them, showing each as a specific bone. Each one is important. The children are an important part of our church too. Ask the children what bone they want to be. Explain the children's importance: they sing for the church, they make church more fun, they will be the future leaders. Show what the skeleton would be like without children. They are one of the bones we need. Each of them is important and belongs here.

Notes: For the skeleton you can use the kind that are Halloween decorations. Halloween is a good time to get one, since they can be hard to find at other times of the year.

If you have access to a real skeleton, such as one that may be used in a classroom, that would be even better.

31. Do You Trust Me?

Theme: Faith means to trust.

Faith is an important concept in Biblical religion, especially for Christians. Paul describes faith as being a cornerstone of our salvation. But faith is also an abstract idea unless it is concretely described in terms of daily life. In this sense, one of the dynamics at work in faith is trust. Those who have faith in God trust God.

Scripture: Psalm 27:14

Device: A blindfold

Goals: To teach the meaning of faith
To experience faith

Technique: This lesson is intended to demonstrate the trust element in faith by challenging the children to trust you, the leader. The analogy can then be drawn between their trust, or faith, in you and their trust, or faith, in God.

Point out to the children that the verse in the psalm (Good News Bible) talks about trusting God and having faith in God. How many of them have heard the word "faith"? What is faith? When we have faith in someone, we trust that person, whether it be God or a human being. How many of the children have someone they trust? What does it mean to trust?

Ask how many of the children trust you. Which ones trust you enough to let you lead them around the church while they are blindfolded? Select a volunteer to be blindfolded, then lead that child around the church. Help the child avoid a few obstacles, such as a piano, or help the blindfolded one through some tricky spots, like some steps. The guided walk is meant to be a demonstration of the child's trust.

After the walk is over, ask the other children if the volunteer showed trust. The answer should be yes. That's what it means to trust someone. The Bible tells us we are to trust God in the same way. Let God guide you and let God protect you. That's what it means to have faith.

Notes: It would be worthwhile, if you have enough time, to let more than one child experience being blindfolded and trusting.

In the appropriate situation, it would be effective to let the children blindfold and lead each other, trusting each other.

32. Blindman's Buff

Theme: Unless we follow Jesus, we're going to get lost.

Jesus described the people of Israel as lost sheep, but that's an accurate description of all people. Humans are largely unable to determine the true direction in which they are moving and the far-reaching consequences of their actions. We are blind, and follow others who are blind. That is disastrous for our lives and for the world. The answer to this situation is to follow Christ, the light of the world. He can see, and with him we are correctly guided.

Scripture: Luke 6:39

Device: Two blindfolds

Goals: To demonstrate the results of blindness and following blindly
To help children experience what it means to be blind or follow blindly
To communicate their need for Jesus

Technique: This lesson allows active participation by some of the children, and lets their participation teach them the message.

After reading the verse of Scripture, ask the children what it means to be blind. Discuss this with them and establish some of the problems that blind people have: becoming lost, tripping on objects, possibly hurting themselves or breaking things. Sometimes blind people have guides, both persons and dogs, to help them avoid these troubles. What would happen if their guide happened to be blind too? The person whom we follow, who guides us, is very important because that individual can protect us or lead us into trouble. Jesus said this.

Cover a volunteer's eyes with a blindfold. Challenge the child to find his or her parents or a friend after being turned around a few times. The child will wander and stumble around, to the great delight of the other children. Ask for a second volunteer to guide the first child. Cover this child's eyes with a blindfold too, and after several turns place the hands of the two children together. Ask the second child to guide the first child to the parents or a friend. Again, the two are unable to do it, to the entertainment of all. Finally, ask a third child, who can see, to guide the two to their goal.

Point out to the children that the two blind volunteers didn't know where they were going. It is important to have someone guide us who can see. Whom does the Bible tell us to follow? Who is our best guide? Jesus! Let's all follow Jesus so that none of us becomes lost.

Notes: This is a good opportunity for you to use an older child, perhaps a boy, who does not usually take an active part in the games or demonstrations. The child will enjoy this.

WORSHIP

33. Praise God

Theme: Praising God can be noisy and fun.

Visit any sports contest and you can hear people expressing praise. Fans yell and stomp their feet, encouraging their teams. Air horns blast. Bands play stirring marches and calls to arms. It is a very different scene from the worship of many churches, in which God is supposedly being praised. However, noisy enthusiasm is O.K. with God. The psalms talk about praising God with trumpets, drums, flutes, and cymbals; especially, says Psalm 150, with loud cymbals. God can be praised in silence and solemnity, but praising God can also be noisy and playful.

Scripture: Psalm 150

Device: Various noisy instruments: drums, tambourines, cymbals, wood blocks, horns

Goals: To teach the children to praise God
To help the children to enjoy praising God

Technique: After reading the psalm, lead the children in a discussion about the meaning of praise. What is praise? Why do we praise God? Explain that this psalm suggests ways in which we can praise God. What were some of the suggestions? You may want to read to the children those particular verses again.

Tell the children that they can praise God just as the

Bible describes. Praising God is part of worship, and that's what you are all going to do. Hand out the instruments, keeping one for yourself. After the children have thought of something for which they are thankful, have them shout hurray for God and play their instruments. Lead the children in three or four rounds of praise.

Notes: Choose instruments that will be easy for the children to use.

As an option, which will provide a follow-up lesson, ask the children to each bring an instrument for the next session. On that day, have the children distribute the instruments among the adults who are present, letting the adults join in the praising.

34. Sing a Song

Theme: Singing is a way to praise God.

Singing praise to God is an ancient way of worshiping. Many of the psalms, which were usually sung or accompanied by music, place song and praise in the same category. In song we can express our thankfulness in words and in feelings.

Scripture: Psalm 147:1

Device: A song

Goals: To teach the purpose of song in worship
To help the children praise God
To have fun

Technique: Review the meaning of praise. Praise is a way of giving thanks to God. How does this psalm say we can praise God? We can do so in song.

Lead the children in a fun song of praise. Children especially like songs that are accompanied by movements. Choose a song that is sung often in Sunday school, or select from the hymnal one that is appealing to children.

Notes: You may want to have the songs accompanied by piano or guitar, since an organ can be overpowering to children.

You can have the children learn the song and then lead the congregation.

35. Praying

Tom Z.
used in CWM 89

Theme: We can pray by holding out our hands and looking upward.

There are different physical attitudes traditionally used for prayer. In many Protestant denominations, however, the posture of a bowed head and clasped hands seems to predominate. This posture is unlike that of the early Christians. They frequently looked upward and held their hands outward in receptivity. Whether praying is done with head bowed or raised; while standing, sitting, or kneeling; with hands clasped or outstretched; in words or in silent meditation—it is important that Christians become comfortable with the varieties of prayer and learn to use them in their lives.

Scripture: Luke 11:1

Device: A demonstration of an early Christian praying

Goals: To teach the meaning of prayer
To teach a different method of prayer
To teach the place of prayer in worship

Technique: Discuss the meaning of prayer with the children. Why do we pray? To whom do we pray? Point out to the children that prayer is a part of worship.

Ask the children how they pray, then explain that Christians who lived long ago often prayed differently. They would look upward instead of bowing their heads. Why would they look up? They imagined God was up there. Instead of clasping their hands, they would hold their hands open and outstretched. Why would they do this? If you were going to receive a gift, would you take it by holding your hands together or holding them outward? The early Christians held their hands outward, expecting to receive something from God. After the explanation, lead the children in this manner of prayer.

Notes: You can point out that there are Christians today who pray in this way.

36. The Treasure Chest

Theme: The Bible has many treasures in it for us to find.

Within the Bible is divine wisdom. It is God's Word for those who can hear that Word. But to understand that Word and to receive God's help we need to study, search, and hold on to what is given. The Bible will reveal its treasures to those who seek for them.

Scripture: Matthew 13:44

Device: A large container filled with sand; a large coin; a key; an imitation jewel

Goals: To teach the purpose of the Bible
To teach the place of the Bible in worship
To make the Bible special

Technique: Review the short parable, making sure the children understand the gist of the story. The man found a treasure, then bought the field so that he could keep the treasure he had found. Draw a parallel between the story and the Bible. The Bible is like that field, and in the Bible are many treasures, if we can find them.

Show the children the container of sand, informing them that some treasures are hidden in the sand. Would anyone like to find one? Let the children, one at a time, dig through the sand until one of the hidden objects has been discovered. Point out that they are treasure hunting, looking for important things that are hidden. This is what we should also do with the Bible. The Bible has treasures in it, like the can of sand, which will help us to be happier. But we must find them. That's why we read the Bible. We hope that God will help us find another treasure in the Bible.

Notes: This is a good lesson to use if you hand out Bibles during church to certain children on a Moving-Up Day, or the equivalent.

37. Kneeling Like Wise Men

Theme: Kneeling is part of worship.

Kneeling is an ancient act of devotion and humility. People in the Bible prostrate themselves, especially in the presence of God, as the Wise Men did before the infant Jesus. Today, in some churches, this practice has been given mainly a vestigial role, exercised, perhaps, in Communion. In so doing, we have missed an elemental aspect of worship and removed this experience from our children.

Kneeling can become a meaningless ritual. Going to the altar is not an unfailing sign of great faith, nor is it necessary for salvation. But it is an important act, which has a great effect on those who do it sincerely. For a more meaningful worship, and a deeper spiritual life, kneeling needs to become more practiced and the altar needs to become more open.

Scripture: Matthew 2:11

Device: An altar railing (if available)

Goals: To open the altar to children
To teach children the use and importance of kneeling
To give children an opportunity to kneel

Technique: Outline enough of Matthew's Christmas story to give the verse a solid context, then read the brief description of what the Wise Men did when they found Jesus. Ask the children to tell you what the men did. The children will surely know that the men gave gifts to the baby. Few or none will understand that the men also knelt before the child.

Tell the children that the Wise Men did kneel, and explain what kneeling is. Children are interested in the origin of kneeling. When a soldier or a servant knelt before a king, and bared the back of the neck, he was making himself defenseless and vulnerable. It was a sign of devotion, because it offered the king an opportunity to cut off the person's head. Though God won't kill us, we still kneel before God to show our love and respect.

Kneeling also needs to be given another purpose. Explain some of the things we may do when we kneel: pray, give thanks to God, or ask for forgiveness. If you wish, have the children think of things for which to thank God or for which to ask forgiveness. After you have done this, ask the children to kneel at the altar railing, if there is one available. Otherwise, they may kneel wherever it is convenient to do so. Tell them to say silently what they want to say to God. Then close with a short, appropriate prayer.

Notes: This is a good lesson to use before asking the children to kneel during a Communion service.

The remarks of the children have led me to believe that this act is very meaningful for them.

MARRIAGE

38. The First Wedding

Theme: God started marriage.

Marriage is a difficult relationship, made more difficult by the ignorance of many people about its nature and purposes. Much more education about marriage needs to be done, especially with children, and Biblical principles concerning marriage need to be taught.

Christian teaching about marriage begins with the belief that marriage is a relationship intended by God between a man and a woman. Marriage, in the traditional wedding ceremony, is described as "instituted of God." God ordained marriage to be an unbreakable, earthly bond that forms the foundation for family life.

Scripture: Mark 10:6–7

Device: A wedding ring

Goals: To teach the nature of marriage
To teach who started marriage
To teach that marriage is sacred

Technique: Most children have been to weddings, and some have been in them. A good introduction to the lesson is to ask the children about weddings they have seen. Who was married? Were they in the wedding? Who married the couple? Did the children see a minister or a priest? Show the children a wedding ring. Did they see the couple put on rings when they were married?

Wearing a wedding ring is a sign that that person is married.

Ask the children to identify the first persons ever to be married. It is Adam and Eve, of course. Who married them? Who made Adam and Eve to be husband and wife? God did that. God started marriage and married the first people. The reason people are married today is that God began marriage a long time ago. When a man and a woman like each other very much, God wants them to become married.

Notes: Be careful that you do not communicate that God wants all people to be married. Jesus tells us that not everyone needs to become married, and that remaining single is acceptable to God.

39. Promises, Promises

Theme: In marriage, the man and the woman make promises to each other.

Marriages are based on sets of agreements or promises that individuals have made to each other. The wedding ceremony and the marriage license are both concerned, in different ways, with these contracts between the man and the woman. When marriages become troubled, or fall apart, it is because some of these promises have not been kept, even though the promises may not have been consciously acknowledged. An important need in marriage is for us to recognize that the marriage is based upon mutual promises, and to recognize what unique sets of promises are being agreed to in each case.

Scripture: Hebrews 13:4

Device: A pair of wedding rings

Goals: To teach the nature of marriage
To teach that married people have made promises to each other

Technique: Again, ask the children if they recognize what type of rings you are holding in your hand. What people do they know who are married? Does their mother or father wear a ring? Have they seen persons being married? What happens at weddings?

Starting with what the children say happens at weddings, explain that individuals make promises to each other at weddings. Do the children know what a promise is? Have them give some examples. Married people make promises too. What promises do the children think married people make? Read the marriage vows to the children and briefly explain them. When the Bible says that husband and wife should be faithful to each other, it means that they should always keep their promises to each other. Divorces happen when the promises between husband and wife are broken. Good marriages happen when the promises are always kept.

Notes: Be prepared to deal with the children who talk about parents who have been divorced. Divorce is a very important issue for children to understand.

COVENANTS

12/30/90

40. The Handshake

Theme: God makes deals with us.

Though it sounds oddly human, the Bible teaches that God makes deals with us. These deals are called covenants in Scripture, and have obligations for both human beings and God. The deal is straightforward in Deuteronomy: if people obey God's laws, God will bless those people with land and prosperity.

Scripture: Deuteronomy 30:16

Device: A handshake

Goals: To teach what a covenant is
To teach about God's covenants
To lead the children into a covenant with God

Technique: Giving a handshake to someone is a com mon practice, and children will most likely have observed it. Ask why people shake hands. Of course, a handshake can be simply a way of saying hello or good-by, but even underlying these forms of greeting there is an agreement taking place between the individuals shaking hands. Lead the discussion to show the children that handshaking can be a way of finalizing deals by "shaking on them." For an example, use a deal that is common between parents and children, such as working for spending money. Make a deal with the children to be friends, and then shake on it with each of them.

Tell the children that God makes deals with us too, and we can shake on it with God. In the Scripture, what does God want us to do? What does God promise to do for us? God will help us to be happy if we do what God says. The more we obey God, the more of God's help we will receive. That's the deal. God makes deals with us, and God will keep his promise if we shake on it with him.

Notes: This lesson can be treated as an introduction to the idea of covenants, or as a summary of previous lessons, or as an opportunity for the children to agree to a covenant with God. They can shake on it with God in prayer.

41. God Never Forgets

Theme: God never forgets his promises.

The conscious and unconscious forgetfulness of people makes trust a difficult quality to develop. We often do not know if people will do what they have promised, or if they will even remember making a promise. Contracts, covenants, and deals can become very twisted once they are consigned to a person's mind and memory. But these are not problems for God. God always remembers. The Bible continually emphasizes that God remembers his deals; it is people who forget them. We can depend upon God to do completely what he has promised.

Scripture: Psalm 111:5

Device: A demonstration of forgetfulness

Goals: To teach what God is like
To teach the nature of God's covenants
To instill in the children trust in God

Technique: A demonstration of forgetfulness can help children learn what it means to always remember. This can be done easily in two ways. You can promise to do something with the children at the next lesson, then purposely forget. That will work if there isn't too much time between the lessons. Or you can begin the lesson with a purposeful show of forgetfulness. Call the children by the wrong names, pretend that you think you're someplace else and that it's a different day. The children will enjoy the demonstration. Explain that you are being forgetful.

Discuss forgetfulness with the children. Do they know anyone who forgets things? Have they themselves ever forgotten something? Has someone ever forgotten a promise to them? Forgetfulness is a problem that people have.

Who never forgets, according to the Bible? God never does. God always remembers; God is not like people. God always remembers who you are. God always remembers what day it is. Whatever you had purposely forgotten earlier in the lesson, point out that God never forgets those things. God never forgets the promises he has made. If God tells you that he will do something, God will always do it. Humans may forget promises, but God never does.

Notes: You can tie this lesson into whatever deals you have already discussed with the children. What particular promise will God never forget?

42. The Old Deal

Theme: The old covenants emphasized obedience.

The divine covenants of the Old Testament focused upon what people had to do, emphasizing obedience to sacred law. That obedience was so difficult that even the most respected figures, such as Moses or David, failed in their attempts and suffered proportionate losses of God's blessings: Moses could not enter the Promised Land, David's family fell apart and turned against him. This system, which focused upon law, obedience, and punishment, was altered by the revelation of God in Jesus.

Scripture: Deuteronomy 30:17–18

Device: Handcuffs

Goals: To teach the meaning of the old covenants
To teach the difference that Christ makes

Technique: This lesson is designed to be used with further sermons about the new covenant made possible by Christ. It presents an ancient view of the God/human relationship that Christ refocused.

Do the children know that the Bible is divided into two parts? What are those two parts? Emphasize the designations "old" and "new." The first part tells about the old deals between people and God. The second part tells about the new deal that God made with people, after Jesus. Today you're going to tell them about the old deals, before Jesus came.

Talk to the children about laws. What is a law? Can they list some laws? What happens if they disobey a law? Give some obvious examples that even small children will understand. If you disobey a law, you may be arrested and handcuffed. Show the handcuffs, explaining how and why they are used. As a punishment, a person may be put in jail. Have the children ever seen a jail? Do they think it is good or bad to be arrested, handcuffed, and put in jail? Handcuffs are for persons who break the law.

Long ago the people thought about their deal with God in the same way. They believed that God made laws. Can the children think of any of God's laws? Like our laws today, the laws of God had to be obeyed. If you obeyed the rules, God would be good to you; if you broke the rules, bad things would happen to you. Give examples, using the laws of God already mentioned. Read the Scripture again, pointing out the penalty for breaking the law. Does that sound good or bad? In the old deal, people thought of God as someone who told them what to do and put handcuffs on those who disobeyed. Holding up the handcuffs, repeat that the old deal was about being good and obeying God's laws, or being punished.

But God wanted to change the way people understood that deal. God wanted to be known as someone who loves people. God wanted to be understood as someone who gives us gifts, not as someone who always threatens to punish. This new understanding was really a new deal. Whom did God send to show the difference between the old deal and the new deal? Jesus shows us God's love. Jesus made clear that the new deal with God sets us free from unnecessary fears of laws and punishments. Tell the children that next time we'll talk about God's new deal in Jesus.

43. The New Deal

Theme: Jesus gives us a new deal with God.

Franklin Delano Roosevelt, our president during the Great Depression, wasn't the only man who ever offered "a new deal." Jesus did too. Thanks to the work of God in Jesus, obedience is no longer a requirement for receiving help from God. Much of God's bounty is given freely, without conditions, and our efforts to obey God can now bring blessings not previously imagined. Jesus has made a tremendous difference. The change between the Old Testament and the New Testament, between the old deal and the new deal, is very large and very real.

Scripture: Romans 3:23–24

Device: Handcuffs; a gift-wrapped box

Goals: To teach the difference that Jesus makes
To teach the meaning of the new deal

Technique: Show the children the handcuffs and review the old deal. What did people have to do? Was it easy? Who changed the old deal? Tell them that today you will talk about how Jesus changed the old deal.

Hold up the gift-wrapped box and discuss the meaning of gifts with the children. What is a gift? When do they receive gifts? Why do people give gifts? Paul says that God's help and love are now free gifts, thanks to Jesus. Do you need to buy a free gift? Do you need to earn a free gift? At Christmas, when we're told to be good or Santa will not come, is that a free gift? Why isn't it?

In the new deal we don't have to be good so that God will be good to us, and our breaking the law won't make

God punish us. Hold up the handcuffs; that's the old deal. In the new deal, God will love us and help us even if we disobey his laws. If we break God's rules, we will hurt ourselves, but God won't hurt us. We can't do anything to make God stop loving us.

The old deal was with God the law giver; hold up the handcuffs. The new deal is with God the gift giver; hold up the gift box. God gives us his love as a free gift. That's the new deal that Jesus brings. Ask the children which deal they think is better. Which do they want for themselves? Why? If the children want the new deal of God's freely given love, they need only to accept the gift and say thank you. Lead them in a prayer of acceptance and thanks. Help the children with what to say, but have them pray for themselves silently. Close by shouting thank you to Jesus.

Notes: This lesson can be adapted to your own particular views about salvation.

You may want to give the children a token signifying that they have received God's gift, such as a tag with the words, "God loves me."

44. Our Father

Theme: Jesus can make God our Father.

Even for many Christians, God is a distant and forbidding figure. While people think of Jesus as a safe, loving person, they maintain a fear of the judging God. The New Testament tells us, however, that there is no difference between the nature of God and the nature of Jesus. God is the safe, loving person we see in Jesus. If we trust Jesus and the image Jesus gives to us, God can be a loving father for us.

Scripture: John 14:6

Device: Fathers in the congregation

Goals: To teach part of the meaning of the new deal
To teach what God can be for us
To help children begin to receive this teaching

Technique: The easiest way to teach about God as our Father is to draw the parallel between God and the highest qualities of fatherhood we see among people. That makes God as a father much more visible.

Ask all the fathers in the congregation to stand up so the children can see them, then talk with the children about fathers. What is a father? What do fathers do? What do the children most like about fathers? Jesus says that God can be a father for us too. Using the qualities the children have just mentioned, and adding what they may have overlooked, describe what God is like as a father. Refer to their own experiences with their own fathers. Would the children like God to be that way?

God can be a father to us. We only need to ask Jesus

for that, because it is part of the new deal that Jesus brings. God will be our Father if we tell Jesus our wish. Close by having the children shake on their deal with Jesus in prayer. Give the children specific words to pray.

Notes: This could be a good lesson to use on Father's Day.

Be prepared for the children to talk about some negative qualities of the fathers they have. It is important for the children to share this, if the situation is appropriate. It is also important to separate God our Father from the weaknesses of human fathers. This is a connection which troubles many people.

45. Dead or Alive?

Theme: Jesus can give us life.

Life is a possession we take too much for granted. We think we are living when the Bible says we are merely existing, an existence that is like death when compared to the life possible through Christ. For children, this is best symbolized as a choice between life and death, which is how the Bible frequently describes it. Jesus offers us life; without him we remain deadened.

Scripture: John 20:31

Device: A pile of dead grass; a clump of live grass

Goals: To teach part of the new deal
To teach the importance of Christ
To show children the choice they have

Technique: Briefly summarize the meaning of the verse by asking the children what it says Jesus can give to us. Right now you want to talk about Jesus and life.

Hold up the two clumps of grass. Ask the children what you are holding and how they differ. How can the children tell which pile is dead and which is alive? Why might the grass have died? Review for the children why the grass died and the implications of being dead. The grass died because it was cut off from its roots and the ground; it had no food. It can't grow anymore, or be happy, or have friends. That's not true for the live grass. It stayed in the ground, where it can be fed and get water. That grass is growing and happy.

Jesus gives us life. That's what the Bible verse says. Jesus is like the ground for us. Demonstrate with the clump of live grass. We must stay with Jesus, attached to him, have our roots in him, as the grass has its roots in the ground. Apart from Jesus we die; we can be alive and happy and growing only when we're with Jesus.

Show them the grasses again. Which do they want to be: the dead brown grass, or the live green grass? If they want to have life, they can make a deal with Jesus. That is part of Christ's new deal. If we follow Jesus and do what he says, Jesus will give us life and help us to be happy.

Notes: This is a good opportunity to lead the children in a prayer of commitment. They can tell Jesus that they want to be alive and happy, and are willing to follow him. Do that in silent prayer, when the children can make their commitment for themselves. Simply make sure the children know what they can say, if they wish.

46. The Rainbow

Theme: The rainbow is a sign of one of God's deals with us.

The rainbow is such a beautiful phenomenon that it seems inevitable to use it as a sign of God's covenant. That is the meaning given to the rainbow in the strange story of Noah. God promises to treat all human beings with kindness, love, and patience, designating a rainbow as the sign of that promise. Whenever we see a rainbow, we can remember that promise, which God has fulfilled in many glorious ways, and which is still in effect.

Scripture: Genesis 9:16–17

Device: A picture of a rainbow

Goals: To teach about God's promise of love
To teach the symbolic meaning of a rainbow
To help children remember God's love for them

Technique: Draw a rainbow or hold up a picture of one. What is it? Have the children discuss what rainbows are and when they have seen them. Point out that God talks about rainbows in the Bible.

God says that the rainbow is a sign of the deals he makes with us and the gifts he gives to us. Can they remember any of those deals? Summarize what you have previously taught, emphasizing the new deal in Christ and God's willingness to help us. Every time we see a rainbow in the sky, we can remember God's promises and that God is kind and will always love us.

Notes: What an opportunity if there is a real rainbow!

BAPTISM

47. Getting Clean

Theme: In baptism God makes us clean.

Water is an element rich in symbolic meaning. It is a symbol of humility, strength, life, and cleansing. The accretions to our lives, caused by sin, are washed away in God's sight in baptism. The water is a symbol of this divine cleansing, marking the beginning of a new life free from any prior stain.

Scripture: Acts 22:16

Device: A small adult doll; a pitcher of water; a basin

Goals: To teach a meaning of baptism
To make a ritual of the church more meaningful

Technique: This lesson demonstrates simply one of the natural symbolic meanings of water. Before the message, roll the small doll in some dirt and place it in the basin. By pouring the water over the doll, in a reenactment of baptism, the children will see the cleansing effect of water and baptism.

Start the children thinking about baptism. How many of them have been baptized? What happens when someone is baptized? Why would we baptize somebody by putting water on the head, or immersing the person? Begin with a simple question and proceed to the more abstract ones, letting the children chew on the problem a little.

The children may very well mention the ability of water to clean things. One child began to describe how her mother used water to give her baths and to wash her hair. If this doesn't happen, ask the children how water is used. Why do we take baths in water? Water is good for cleaning things. In baptism, God uses water to clean us.

Hold up the doll covered with dirt. Just as we need to take baths to keep our bodies clean, we need God to make us clean from our sins. God cleans us in baptism. Pour the water from the pitcher over the doll. The water will wash the dirt from the doll into the basin. Hold up the clean doll, showing the children how the water has removed all the dirt. Baptizing a baby or an adult with water is a way to show that God cleans us from all the bad things we have done or ever will do.

Notes: In the baptism ritual, it is helpful to emphasize the presence of water. In the sprinkling forms of baptism this can be done by publicly pouring the water into the font.

If you have the children remain to watch a baptism, be sure to tell them to sit quietly.

I think a small adult doll is better than a baby doll because it is less likely to communicate that only children are dirty.

48. Getting Watered

Theme: Baptism reminds us that God keeps us alive.

Water is necessary for life. Water is found wherever life is found, so that the two become nearly synonymous. As such, water becomes a symbol of God's creative and sustaining powers. Being touched by water is like being touched by God and his divine powers.

Scripture: Acts 8:12

Device: A potted plant; two pitchers, one containing water

Goals: To teach a meaning of baptism

Technique: After telling the children that there will be a baptism, ask them what happens in baptism. What is put on the person's head or what is the person immersed in? Have the children focus on the water.

Water is an important element. What happens when we don't have water? Pour water from one pitcher to another so the children can see some water. What would happen to this plant if it didn't have water? It would die. We would die too, like the plant, if we didn't have water. Everyone needs water to live. Pour water on the plant, repeating that water keeps us alive.

Who gives us the water? God does. God gives us water so that we'll live. Pour water on the plant again and repeat that God keeps us alive. Baptism, either by touching a person's head with water or immersing the person, is a way of remembering that God keeps us alive, just as God waters the plants.

Notes: Pouring water into the baptismal font, as you poured it onto the plant, can tie the lesson more closely to the ceremony.

49. One of Us

Theme: In baptism, a person joins the family of Christians.

Initiation rites have existed since the beginning of human civilization. Like keys for a locked door, they are ceremonies that allow a person to enter into a group that otherwise is closed. Baptism is the initiatory rite for Christianity and ceremonially admits a person into the family of believers. It is an act of joy in receiving another person into fellowship.

Scripture: 1 Corinthians 12:13

Device: The congregation

Goals: To teach a meaning of baptism
To give a sense of belonging to the church

Technique: Since baptism is an infrequent ritual, it is necessary each time to introduce the ceremony to the children by discussing the basic facts. What happens at a baptism? What element is used? Have they been baptized? Once the children understand clearly what will soon happen, lead them in a lesson that teaches one of baptism's meanings.

Talk to the children about their families. How many of them belong to a family? What is a family? How did they join their family? Draw a parallel between their family and the family of Christians. The church is a family too.

Ask everyone who has been baptized to stand up. This will include people who may not be members of the church. Explain to the children that all those people are one large family. God is their Father and Mother; they all are brothers and sisters. Baptism has made them members of that family. Baptism is how we join this large family in church; it's how we are born into the church family.

If the children have been baptized already, have them look at the standing congregation and tell them that they belong to that group. Those people in the congregation are their older brothers and sisters. For children who have not been baptized, explain to them that they can become members of that large family when they are baptized. Make sure they know that baptism is available to them, either now or in the future. They can be baptized, the same as the person you will baptize today, and brought into this wonderful group of people who love one another.

Notes: Adapt this lesson to your own baptismal practices. If you have a believer's baptism, explain to the children when baptism will be available to them.

As a complement to this lesson, try to emphasize the elements in the baptism ritual that deal with admission into the family of believers.

COMMUNION

50. In Remembrance

Theme: Communion is a time to remember Jesus.

Communion is a ritual based upon remembering Jesus. We are to think about Christ, and his meaning for our lives, as we share the bread and wine (or juice). What did he do? What has he done for you?

Scripture: Luke 22:19

Device: Communion elements; a dialogue

Goals: To teach a meaning of Communion
To include children meaningfully in the Sacrament
To remember what Jesus has done for us

Technique: Read the section on Communion for children in the Introduction.

Introduce the Communion meal with a discussion about remembering Jesus. What does it mean to remember somebody? Ask the children what they can remember about Jesus, and amplify. If they remember Jesus as doing good things, have them be more specific. What good things? If the children remember that Jesus loves them, emphasize this, pointing out individual children as examples of people whom Jesus loves. During Communion we are to remember and think about Jesus.

After some remembrance of Jesus has taken place,

share the elements with the children. As you give them the bread and wine, recite the good things of Jesus which they have mentioned. Repeat his love for each child by name as you serve that child.

51. The Greatest Gift

Theme: Communion is a time to remember that Jesus died for us.

As Jesus inaugurates the ritual of Communion, he emphasizes that the rite will be an act for remembering his sacrificial death. Jesus gave his life for us, for friends and foes alike. As Jesus says, there can be no greater love than this.

Scripture: John 15:13

Device: Communion elements; a cross

Goals: To teach the meanings of Communion
To include children meaningfully in Communion
To make the death of Jesus more personal

Technique: The purpose of this lesson is to bring the death of Jesus, his greatest act of love, to the children's attention at Communion. By teaching the children that Communion is a time to remember this sacrifice, and then helping them to remember, Communion can be made meaningful. At the same time, the death of Jesus can be made more personal for each child.

After reading the Scripture, ask the children if they know what it means to "give your life" for someone. One of the older children is likely to know. Place that in the context of giving a gift. All of us give gifts to other people. How many of us would give our life for someone? How many of us would die for someone else? I have yet to find a child who says he or she would. Jesus says that is the greatest gift of love that can be given, and it is what Jesus did. Jesus died for us so that we can have eternal life. Point to the cross and ask who died on it. The children will know that Jesus did. Affirm their answer, and repeat that Jesus died for them because he loves them so much. Communion is a time to remember that Jesus died for us.

Invite the children to kneel at the altar, and distribute the elements to them. For each child, repeat the message about Jesus' sacrifice. During Communion we remember that Jesus died on the cross. To make this gift even more personal, include the name of each child, if you know it. "Jesus died on the cross for David. This bread is like his body which was killed. This juice is like his blood."

Notes: Refer to the section on Communion for children in the Introduction.

The lesson "Kneeling Like Wise Men" could be useful before having the children kneel for Communion.

Do not be afraid to make the children be still and treat the altar seriously. If children are starting to climb on the rail, or hang over its edge, simply ask them in a pleasant and firm manner to please stop. You may have to show the children what you want them to do.

52. The Body

Theme: In Communion we remember that the body of Jesus was hurt and killed.

Jesus says that the bread of Communion represents his body given for us. Like the broken bread, his body was broken by the crucifixion, causing him to die. In Communion we are to remember that Jesus allowed his body to be injured and killed on our behalf.

Scripture: 1 Corinthians 11:23–24

Device: Communion elements; a crucifix

Goals: To teach a meaning of Communion
To teach the symbolism of the bread
To make Christ's death more real and personal

Technique: A crucifix can seem like a grisly reminder of Christ's sacrifice, but when that is our purpose it can be a useful symbol. It is a picture that fascinates children, and is often one of the first things they remember about Jesus.

Ask the children how many of them have bodies. Draw their attention to the fact that all of us have bodies and that Jesus did too. One of the things which happens to bodies is that they get hurt. Have the children's bodies ever been hurt? What was the worst thing that ever happened to them? Have they ever broken a bone or had an operation? Discuss with them the pain and fear that can come with a body injury.

Tell the children that Jesus was hurt badly once, too. Do they know how? They will know this. Show them the crucifix. Explain to them that Jesus was crucified and what crucifixion means. Whipping a body and nailing it to a piece of wood are awful things to do to a body. Jesus died because of it. If the children can remember how their bodies have hurt sometimes, they can also know how Jesus felt. But Jesus let himself be hurt and killed so that we would hurt less. The Communion bread makes us think of Jesus' hurt body. We break the bread the way his body was broken. Break the bread to demonstrate.

Ask the children to kneel at the altar for Communion. Show them the bread and the crucifix. When we eat the bread we remember the body of Jesus. Jesus let his body be hurt to help us. When we drink the juice or wine we remember that his hurts made Jesus bleed. As you serve the children, remind them of these meanings. Intersperse this by saying that Jesus let himself be hurt because he loves them.

Notes: Refer to the section on Communion for children in the Introduction.

53. The Blood

Theme: In Communion we remember that Jesus bled for us.

The Communion elements, as stated by Jesus, represent his body and blood. Both have many symbolic meanings, but, in a simple way, both can also help the death of Christ to be more real. We all have bled, we know the experience, and we all can identify with it. This helps us to remember Christ's death as he wished.

Scripture: Mark 14:23–24

Device: Communion elements

Goals: To teach a meaning of Communion
To teach the symbolism of the juice or wine
To make Christ's death more real and personal

Technique: Our own blood is a built-in device for this demonstration. By showing children some blood, we can easily help them to remember times when they have also bled, and more closely identify with Jesus in his death.

After reading the Scripture, talk to the children about blood. What is it? Where does it come from? Show the children some blood to make this discussion more tangible. You can do this in various ways. Pressing down upon your fingertip brings blood to the surface which can be seen through the skin. That is a demonstration which can be done by all the children. If you feel adventurous, while pressing down upon your fingertip, prick it with a pin. Not much squeezing is necessary to force out a drop of blood for display. Another idea is to use the Red Cross Blood Donor badge, which is a drawing of a drop of blood. Use whatever means is most appealing to you.

Make this topic more personal by asking the children if they have ever bled. When? This will be a popular subject, as all children not only have bled but have found the experience very scary, mysterious, and exciting. As they recount their own incidents, and their own fear or pain, tie the stories into the experience of Jesus. Jesus bled when he was nailed to the cross. Jesus was willing to be crucified, and to bleed, in order to help us. The Communion juice helps us to remember that. Show the children the similarity between the wine, or juice, and blood. This is the blood of Jesus.

Invite the children to the altar and serve Communion. Hold up the elements before distribution and remind the children what they are. Repeat the message as you serve the children.

Notes: Refer to the section on Communion for children in the Introduction.

If you use a pin, sterilize it first to avoid infection. If you practice, you'll find that drawing the blood is not difficult or painful; it's just scary to anticipate.

54. Heavenly Food

Theme: In Communion we take Jesus into ourselves.

A balanced diet is always a keystone whenever basic necessities for health are discussed. But fewer people realize that spiritual food is just as necessary for an individual's health, and for a balanced diet, as physical food. Happiness is not possible if our spirits are starving. Jesus is such food, and describes himself that way. When we feed on Jesus, and take him into ourselves, we will be nourished in a very important, and often-neglected, manner. Communion is a ritual in which we take Jesus into ourselves.

Scripture: John 6:35

Device: Communion elements

Goals: To teach a meaning of Communion
To teach who Jesus is
To share Communion meaningfully with the children

Technique: Talk to the children about food and hunger. Do they know when they are hungry? How do they know? What happens when a person doesn't have enough to eat? Can that person be happy when hungry? Food is very important, because it keeps us alive, and we're unhappy when we don't have enough.

In order to be happy we also need to have Jesus in us. Jesus is food for us too, and when Jesus is inside us he can help us in many ways. Jesus says he is like bread. Show the children the Communion bread. As we do with bread, we can take Jesus inside us. Eat some of the bread.

Once Jesus is inside us, he stays there and helps to make us happy.

That is what we do in Communion. Jesus is the bread, and we eat the bread, taking Jesus into our bodies. Jesus is inside us, and that's where we need him to be.

Notes: If you normally use wafers, you might consider using bread this time so that it will fit into the image that Jesus gives to us.

INDEX

Scripture Passages

	Lesson
OLD TESTAMENT	
Genesis 2:24	27
Genesis 9:16–17	46
Deuteronomy 30:16	40
Deuteronomy 30:17–18	42
Psalm 27:14	31
Psalm 109:22	9
Psalm 111:5	41
Psalm 147:1	34
Psalm 150	33
Ecclesiastes 3:5	12
Ecclesiastes 3:6	2
Zechariah 8:16	28
NEW TESTAMENT	
Matthew 2:1	21
Matthew 2:11	37
Matthew 5:9	5
Matthew 5:44	4
Matthew 7:7	11
Matthew 7:14	29
Matthew 13:44	36
Matthew 18:10	15

Matthew 18:12–14   14
Matthew 22:37–39   8
Matthew 28:5–6   23
Mark 10:6–7   38
Mark 14:23–24   53
Luke 2:6–7   22
Luke 6:39   32
Luke 11:1   35
Luke 22:19   50
John 3:16   17
John 6:35   54
John 14:6   44
John 14:9   19
John 14:27   6
John 15:13   51
John 20:31   45
Acts 8:12   48
Acts 22:16   47
Romans 3:23–24   43
Romans 12:4–5   30
1 Corinthians 3:16–17   10
1 Corinthians 11:23–24   52
1 Corinthians 12:13   49
1 Corinthians 13:4   13
1 Corinthians 15:22   24
2 Corinthians 9:15   16
2 Corinthians 13:11   3
Galatians 5:14   7
Ephesians 1:1   1
Ephesians 6:1   25
Colossians 1:15   18
Colossians 3:20   26
Hebrews 1:3   20
Hebrews 13:4   39